WOULD YOU RATHER BOOK FOR KIDS

VALENTINE'S DAY EDITION

Sweet & Silly Valentine's Day Questions for Kids Ages 7-13

This Book Belongs to

_____

_____

Thanks!

Thank you for your purchase. If you enjoyed this book, please consider dropping us a review. It takes only 5 seconds and helps small independent publishers like ours.

Scripto Love
PRESS

Copyright © 2024 Scripto Love Press

All rights reserved. This book, or parts thereof, may not be reproduced in any form without the written permission of the copyright holder.

WOULD YOU RATHER BOOK FOR KIDS: VALENTINE'S DAY EDITION

Spot illustrations: Freepik.com & MidJourney.com

CONTENTS

Introduction v

Valentine's Day
Would You Rather FAQs vii

1. Sweetheart Scenarios 1

2. Candy Kisses 19

3. Fanciful Flowers 35

4. Hearty Conundrums 51

INTRODUCTION

Welcome to the delightful world of "Would You Rather Book for Kids: Valentine's Day Edition." This heartwarming and joyous book brings forth a bouquet of Valentine-themed dilemmas, inviting children to make choices as sweet as a box of chocolates. With sweetheart scenarios and cupid conundrums, it encourages kids to hone their decision-making skills while serving up extra doses of Valentine's Day cheer. Ideal for parties, sleepovers, game nights, vacations, or road trips, and even perfect for solitary play! Whatever you choose, get ready for a fantastically "hearty" time!

VALENTiNE'S DAY WOULD YOU RATHER FAQs

Hey there, Valentine's Day enthusiasts! We've got answers to your hearty questions about our awesome game.

HOW MANY PLAYERS?
You need at least two players, but the more, the merrier! If you have a big group, consider splitting into smaller ones for maximum fun.

WHO GOES FIRST?
To kick things off, let's get creative! The player born closest to Valentine's Day gets the honor of starting the game.

HOW TO PLAY?
First, you'll need your questions. Each player takes turns picking a random question from the book. The first player asks it to someone

(or everyone), and play continues clockwise. (Don't forget to ask *why* they chose the answer they did.) Keep going until all questions are answered or it's time for more celebrating!

IS THERE A TIME LIMIT?

It's your call. If you want to speed things up and add some excitement, set a timer. Quick answers can be hilarious, especially for the super-silly questions!

Valentine's Day just got sweeter and more fun!

1
SWEETHEART SCENARIOS

Would you rather receive Valentine's chocolates from your teacher

or

no homework for a week from your teacher?

Would you rather receive a card with a poem written inside

or

a card filled with humorous jokes and puns?

Would you rather create handmade Valentine's Day cards for all your friends

or

decorate heart-shaped cookies together?

Would you rather create
a 3D valentine card

or

a card with a beautiful calligraphy
message for your Valentine?

Would you rather have a
valentine card with a heartfelt
handwritten letter

or

a card with a collage of your
memorable pictures together
on Valentine's Day?

Would you rather receive
a valentine card filled with
colorful illustrations

or

one with elegant black and white
designs for Valentine's Day?

Would you rather receive a
valentine card that lights up

or

one with a scented element
on Valentine's Day?

Would you rather design
a valentine card with
a hidden message

or

one with a puzzle to solve
for your valentine?

Would you rather receive a funny comic strip valentine card

or

one illustrated with a love story for Valentine's Day?

Would you rather have a valentine card that includes a small gift attached

or

a card with a scratch-off message for Valentine's Day?

Would you rather create a valentine card filled with your favorite memories

or

one expressing your dreams for the future with your valentine?

Would you rather receive
a card with an original song lyric

or

a card with meaningful quotes
on Valentine's Day?

Would you rather have a
valentine card with a story
about your relationship

or

a card with a map showing
your favorite places together?

Would you rather receive
a valentine card with a
personalized crossword puzzle

or

a card with a series of riddles
to decipher on Valentine's Day?

Would you rather create a Valentine's Day card with glitter

or

one filled with colorful stickers?

Would you rather design a card with a cute animal drawing

or

one with a magical unicorn illustration for Valentine's Day?

Would you rather make a card with a sweet message

or

a card that tells a story about your friendship for Valentine's Day?

Would you rather design a card that shows your favorite outdoor activity

or

one with your favorite indoor game for Valentine's Day?

Would you rather create a card with a superhero theme

or

one with a magical castle for Valentine's Day?

Would you rather receive a card that smells like your favorite fruit

or

one that smells like fresh flowers for Valentine's Day?

Would you rather make a card shaped like your favorite animal

or

one shaped like a heart for Valentine's Day?

Would you rather design a card with a picture of your dream adventure

or

one with a picture of your dream vacation spot for Valentine's Day?

Would you rather create a card with a funny comic strip

or

one with a picture of your favorite board game for Valentine's Day?

Would you rather receive a card with a rainbow theme

or

one filled with your favorite emojis for Valentine's Day?

Would you rather make a card with a jungle animal theme

or

one with a space adventure theme for Valentine's Day?

Would you rather design a card with a picture of your favorite dessert

or

one with a picture of your favorite pet for Valentine's Day?

Would you rather create a card that turns into a mini-book

or

one that turns into a puzzle for Valentine's Day?

Would you rather receive a valentine card with a magical wand illustration

or

one with a pirate treasure map for Valentine's Day?

Would you rather make a card with your favorite sport theme

or

one with a picture of your favorite superhero for Valentine's Day?

Would you rather receive a card with a fairy tale story

or

one with a space adventure story for Valentine's Day?

Would you rather design a valentine card with a picture of your favorite vehicle

or

one with a picture of your dream home for Valentine's Day?

Would you rather create a card with a picture of your favorite season

or

one with a picture of your dream holiday destination for Valentine's Day?

Would you rather make a card with a secret code message

or

one that includes a tiny surprise gift for Valentine's Day?

Would you rather valentine card with a picture of your favorite flower

or

one with your favorite animal for Valentine's Day?

Would you rather create a card with a picture of your favorite food

or

one with a picture of your favorite book for Valentine's Day?

Would you rather make a valentines card with a picture of your favorite superhero

or

one with a picture of your dream vacation for Valentine's Day?

Would you rather receive a card with a picture of your favorite fruit

or

one with a picture of your favorite candy for Valentine's Day?

Would you rather design a card with a picture of your pet

or

one with a picture of your favorite movie character?

Would you rather create a card with a picture of your favorite ice cream flavor

or

one with a picture of your favorite pizza for Valentine's Day?

Would you rather design a card with a picture of your favorite sport

or

one with a picture of your favorite TV show for Valentine's Day?

Would you rather receive a valentine card with a picture of your favorite bird

or

one with a picture of your favorite animal from the zoo for Valentine's Day?

Would you rather design a valentine card with a picture of your dream treehouse

or

one with a picture of your dream vehicle for Valentine's Day?

Would you rather make a card with a picture of your favorite friend

or

one with a picture of your favorite wild animal for Valentine's Day?

Would you rather receive a card with a picture of your favorite ice cream shop

or

one with a picture of your favorite amusement park ride for Valentine's Day?

2
CANDY KISSES

Would you rather receive a heart shaped pizza

or

a heart shaped box of chocolates on Valentine's Day?

Would you rather receive a big box of heart-shaped candies

or

a bag of your favorite chocolates on Valentine's Day?

Would you rather eat 100 conversation hearts

or

100 chocolate kisses?

Would you rather get Valentine's candy from your teacher

or

get a homework pass from your teacher?

Would you rather receive a surprise bouquet of balloons

or

a surprise delivery of your favorite dessert on Valentine's Day?

Would you rather go to a Valentine's Day party with good food but not much else to do

or

go to a Valentine's Day party with no food, but with lots of fun games and activities?

Would you rather eat only red foods on Valentine's Day

or

eat only white foods on Valentine's Day?

Would you rather eat a box full of chocolate covered broccoli

or

a box full of chocolate covered brussel sprouts?

Would you rather make heart-shaped pancakes

or

heart-shaped sandwiches for a special Valentine's Day breakfast?

Would you rather have a Valentine's Day picnic in the backyard

or

a special lunch at your favorite restaurant?

Would you rather receive a heart-shaped box filled with assorted candies

or

a box of your favorite cookies on Valentine's Day?

Would you rather have a Valentine's Day-themed baking competition

or

a Valentine's Day-themed arts and crafts contest?

Would you rather receive a surprise delivery of cupcakes

or

surprise delivery of cute stuffed teddy bears?

Would you rather receive a box of assorted chocolates

or

a giant chocolate bar for Valentine's Day?

Would you rather have dark chocolate truffles

or

milk chocolate-covered strawberries on Valentine's Day?

Would you rather receive heart shaped gummy candies

or

heart shaped cookies on Valentine's Day?

Would you rather receive a box of chocolates filled with various flavors

or

a box of chocolates filled only with your favorite filling?

Would you rather have a chocolate fountain with dippable treats

or

a nacho cheese fountain with assorted dippable treats for Valentine's Day?

Would you rather receive a box of heart-shaped chocolates

or

a box of chocolates in different shapes and sizes for Valentine's Day?

Would you rather have conversation heart candies with personalized messages

or

heart-shaped lollipops for Valentine's Day?

Would you rather have a bag of sour candies

or

sweet chocolates as your Valentine's Day treat?

Would you rather receive a gift basket filled with various types of candies

or

a box of your favorite candy bars for Valentine's Day?

Would you rather receive flowers with a surprise candy assortment

or

flowers with a box of your favorite chocolates on Valentine's Day?

Would you rather have a valentine's box filled with chocolates and a single rose

or

a bouquet of flowers and a box of gourmet chocolate bars for Valentine's Day?

Would you rather have heart-shaped jellybeans

or

heart-shaped marshmallows as your Valentine's Day sweet treat?

Would you rather eat
chocolate covered pickles

or

chocolate covered tomatoes
for Valentine's Day?

Would you rather eat
a chocolate covered onion

or

chocolate covered garlic
for Valentine's Day?

Would you rather eat nothing but chocolate

or

nothing but strawberries for Valentine's Day?

WOuld you rather give up chocolate for six months

or

pizza for six months?

Would you rather give your crush a candy heart

or

give that same person a Hershey kiss?

Would you rather give your teacher a single red rose

or

give your teacher a box of candy?

Would you rather eat a pint of your favorite ice cream

or

a box of chocolates on Valentine's Day?

Would you rather have a dozen heart-shaped cupcakes

or

a single heart-shaped cake on Valentine's Day?

Would you rather eat eggs mixed with small candy hearts

or

mac n' cheese mixed with rose petals?

Would you rather eat a pizza with valentine chocolates on top

or

pasta with caramel covered meatballs on Valentine's Day?

Would you rather eat chocolate covered string beans

or

chocolate covered brussel sprouts on Valentine's Day?

Would you rather eat chocolate covered broccoli

or

chocolate covered kale on Valentine's Day?

Would you rather eat chocolate covered pizza

or

chocolate covered french fries on Valentine's Day?

3
FANCIFUL FLOWERS

Would you rather receive a bouquet of roses

or

a bouquet of your favorite flowers on Valentine's Day?

Would you rather receive a surprise bouquet of balloons

or

a surprise delivery of your favorite dessert on Valentine's Day?

Would you rather receive a surprise delivery of heart-shaped balloons

or

a bouquet of your favorite flowers on Valentine's Day?

Would you rather receive a bouquet of classic red roses

or

a bouquet of mixed colorful flowers on Valentine's Day?

Would you rather have a single long-stemmed rose

or

a bouquet of wildflowers on Valentine's Day?

Would you rather receive a potted plant that blooms all year

or

a fresh bouquet of seasonal flowers for Valentine's Day?

Would you rather have a bouquet of scented flowers

or

a bouquet of flowers with vibrant colors on Valentine's Day?

Would you rather receive a bouquet of your favorite flowers

or

a bouquet that includes a variety of exotic blooms for Valentine's Day?

Would you rather have a bouquet of flowers

or

a box of assorted chocolates for Valentine's Day?

Would you rather receive a bouquet of colorful daisies

or

a bouquet of bright sunflowers for Valentine's Day?

Would you rather have a small potted plant

or

a bouquet of wildflowers for Valentine's Day?

Would you rather receive a bouquet of flowers made of cookies

or

a bouquet of flowers made of chocolate?

Would you rather receive a bouquet of beautiful flowers with no scent

or

an average bouquet of flowers that smell amazing?

Would you rather have a bouquet of flowers that can change their scent

or

flowers that can change their colors for Valentine's Day?

Would you rather have a bouquet of flowers that dance

or

flowers that can make music for Valentine's Day?

Would you rather have a cute little bouquet of flowers

or

a giant bouquest of flowers for Valentine's Day?

Would you rather receive flowers that are magical and make wishes come true

or

flowers that can turn into your favorite animals for Valentine's Day?

Would you rather have a bouquet of flowers that can grow in shapes

or

flowers that can create beautiful patterns in the air for Valentine's Day?

Would you rather receive a bouquet of flowers with shiny petals

or

flowers with sparkles on them for Valentine's Day?

Would you rather receive flowers that can change their size

or

flowers that can magically light up for Valentine's Day?

Would you rather have flowers that can change their scent

or

flowers that can turn into a beautiful rainbow for Valentine's Day?

Would you rather have a bouquet of flowers that can change their appearance

or

flowers that can make you laugh whenever you're sad?

Would you rather receive flowers that can create beautiful music

or

flowers that can change their colors for Valentine's Day?

Would you rather have flowers that can grant you three wishes

or

a bouquet that can make you invisible for Valentine's Day?

Would you rather receive flowers that can bring good luck

or

flowers that can make all your dreams come true for Valentine's Day?

Would you rather have a bouquet of flowers that can create beautiful music

or

a bouquet that can take you on adventures for Valentine's Day?

Would you rather have beautiful flowers that smell like onions

or

a bag of onions that smell like a fresh bouquet of flowers for Valentine's Day?

Would you rather receive flowers that can turn into your favorite sweets

or

flowers that can make the world a happier place for Valentine's Day?

Would you rather have flowers that can grant you magical powers

or

flowers that can grant you unlimited wishes for Valentine's Day?

Would you rather receive a bouquet made of candy

or

a bouquet made of chocolate?

Would you rather receive a bouquet of flowers that smell like your favorite candies

or

flowers that light up like a Christmas tree?

Would you rather create a flower crown made of roses

or

a bracelet made of tiny forget-me-nots for Valentine's Day?

Would you rather spend a day painting a mural filled with yur favorite flowers

or

a day planting your own flower garden?

Would you rather receive a bouquet of roses

or

a bouquet of sunflowers for Valentine's Day?

Would you rather receive a bouquet of roses

or

a bouquet of assorted wildflowers for Valentine's Day?

Would you rather receive a bouquet of red roses

or

a bouquet of white roses?

4
HEARTY CONUNDRUMS

Would you rather skip Halloween **or** skip Valentine's Day?

Would you rather meet Cupid **or** the Easter Bunny?

Would you rather get a lot of valentines from people you don't know very well **or** get just one from someone who is special to you?

Would you rather receive a handmade gift from your valentine

or

a gift purchased from a store?

Would you rather receive 100 little teddy bears

or

1 GIANT teddy bear on Valentine's Day?

Would you rather host a Valentine's Day party

or

be a guest at a Valentine's Day party?

Would you rather write and perform a song for your valentine

or

have your valentine write and perform a song for you on Valentine's Day?

Would you rather receive a romantic piece of artwork

or

a personalized photo album capturing your special moments together?

Would you rather have a long, heartfelt conversation with your valentine

or

enjoy a fun-filled day of activities together on Valentine's Day?

Would you rather spend Valentine's Day with your family

or

spend Valentine's Day with your friends?

Would you rather receive a very special Valentine's Day gift

or

give a very special Valentine's Day gift?

Would you rather get a Valentine's Day kiss from a big, slobbery dog

or

get a Valentine's Day kiss from a grumpy cat?

Would you rather receive a surprise delivery of your favorite books

or

free tickets to your favorite movie for Valentine's Day?

Would you rather have to always write with a red pen

or

dot all of your "i"s and "j"s with hearts for the rest of your life?

Would you rather have a Valentine's Day treasure hunt

or

play Valentine's Day-themed games with your friends?

Would you rather spend Valentine's Day on a roller coaster of love

or

a gentle boat ride on a river of hearts?

Would you rather receive a Valentine's Day-themed coloring book

or

a set of markers and crayons to create your own drawings?

Would you rather receive a magic wand that makes hearts appear

or

a cape that makes you super kind on Valentine's Day?

Would you rather have a valentine-themed treasure hunt

or

a day full of crafting Valentine's Day decorations?

Would you rather have Cupid's magical bow and arrow to make anyone fall in love with you

or

have the power to create the perfect romantic setting instantly?

Would you rather shoot Cupid's magical bow

or

be shot by Cupid's bow?

Would you rather fly with wings like Cupid

or

fly on a broom like a witch?

Would you rather spend the day dressed as Cupid

or

dressed as a bouquet of flowers?

Would you rather spend the day dressed as Cupid

or

a heart-shaped box of chocolates?

Would you rather your breath always smell like roses

or

a box of assorted chocolate?

Would you rather tell your crush you like them

or

have to solve 100 math problems for homework?

Would you rather laugh uncontrollably in front of your crush

or

burst into tears uncontrollably in front of your crush?

Would you rather tell your crush you like them

or

read your journal in front of the entire school?

Would you rather tell your crush you like them

or

be your school's janitor for a week?

Would you rather have a secret admirer

or

be a secret admirer?

Would you rather tell your crush you like them

or

accidentally fart in front of your crush?

Would you rather tell your crush you like them

or

slip and fall in front of your crush?

Would you rather tell your crush you like them

or

have to sing and dance in front of the entire school?

Would you rather have to give up Valentine's Day

or

St. Patrick's Day?

Would you rather have to give up Valentine's Day

or

the 4th of July?

Would you rather have to give up Valentine's Day

or

Memorial Day?

Would you rather eat only chocolate covered cherries for a week

or

conversation heart candies?

Would you rather spend the rest of your life dressed as Cupid

or

dressed as the Easter Bunny?

Would you rather spend the day playing with a dozen puppies

or

playing with a dozen kittens?

Would you rather have to hug everyone you meet

or

sing a love song to everyone you meet?

Would you rather spend the day speaking in rhymes

or

spend the day having to sing everything you say?

Would you rather wear only pink clothes ever again

or

nothing but red clothes?

Would you rather spend the day dressed as Cupid

or

spend the day dressed as a fuzzy teddy bear?

Would you rather spend the rest of your life dressed as Cupid

or

dressed as a mummy?

Would you rather spend the rest of your life dressed as Cupid

or

dressed as a ghost?

Would you rather spend the rest of your life dressed as Cupid

or

dressed as a pilgrim?

Would you rather receive a Valentine's Day card covered in slime

or

one with fake bugs inside?

Would you rather have a box of chocolates filled with flavors like broccoli

or

flavors like pickles for Valentine's Day?

Would you rather have a Valentine's Day-themed slime-making competition

or

a competition to create the grossest-looking edible treat?

Would you rather have a Valentine's Day cake that's decorated with fake vomit

or

a cake that's made to look like slimy bugs?

Would you rather have a dinner with spaghetti that looks like worms

or

a sandwich that looks like it's made of bugs on Valentine's Day?

Would you rather receive a bouquet of flowers that look like weeds

or

a bouquet that smells like stinky cheese for Valentine's Day?

Would you rather spend Valentine's Day searching for hidden surprises in slimy goo

or

in a box filled with fake creepy crawlies?

Would you rather have a Valentine's Day-themed game that involves popping fake pimples

or

a game that involves picking fake boogers?

Would you rather have a Valentine's Day scavenger hunt where you find items hidden in sticky substances

or

items hidden in fake vomit?

Would you rather receive a Valentine's Day gift wrapped in toilet paper

or

wrapped in fake spider webs?

Would you rather receive a Valentine's Day toy that squirts fake snot

or

a toy that makes funny fart noises?

Would you rather receive a Valentine's Day gift that's covered in fake dirt

or

a gift that's covered in fake bugs?

Would you rather have a Valentine's Day snack that looks like it's made of eyeballs

or

a snack that looks like it's made of worms?

Would you rather have your crush give you a special nickname

or

write a song about you for Valentine's Day?

Would you rather receive a Valentine's Day present that's wrapped in wrapping paper covered in bugs

or

in wrapping paper covered in slime?

Would you rather spend Valentine's Day watching a movie with scenes of fake monster creatures

or

scenes with lots of fake slime?

Would you rather have a Valentine's Day dessert that looks like it's covered in fake bugs

or

a dessert that looks like it's covered in fake blood?

Would you rather receive a Valentine's Day card with a funny gross joke

or

a card that has a squishy, gross texture?

Would you rather spend Valentine's Day baking treats together with your crush

or

going on an adventure somewhere new?

Would you rather have your crush tell you a secret on Valentine's Day

or

have them share their favorite things with you?

Would you rather receive a Valentine's Day gift that's meaningful but not expensive

or

something expensive but not very meaningful from your crush?

Would you rather have your crush give you a big smile

or

give you a special compliment on Valentine's Day?

Would you rather have your crush give you a valentine

or

give you a small gift on Valentine's Day?

Made in the USA
Middletown, DE
31 January 2024

48847687R00051